CARING FOR
MY NEW
TURTLE

John Bankston

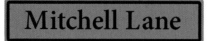

PUBLISHERS

2001 SW 31st Avenue
Hallandale, FL 33009
www.mitchelllane.com

~~~~~~~~~~~~~~~~~~~~~~~~~~~~~~~~~~~~~

First Edition, 2021.

Author: John Bankston
Designer: Ed Morgan
Editor: Morgan Brody

Names/credits:
Title: Caring for My New Turtle / by John Bankston
Description: Hallandale, FL : Mitchell Lane Publishers

Series: How to Care for Your New Pet

Library bound ISBN: 978-1-58415-188-3

eBook ISBN: 978-1-58415-167-8

Photo credits: Freepik.com, Shutterstock

CONTENTS

Words in **bold** throughout can
be found in the Glossary.

Turtle Tales

Did you want a turtle after reading *Tales of a Fourth Grade Nothing*?

The book was about a boy named Peter who had a turtle. He wanted a dog. You should only get a turtle if you really want one.

Ads for turtles once ran in comic books. Children got free turtles by buying a turtle home. Pet turtles were mailed in tiny boxes. Their new owners did not know how to take care of them. The turtles did not live very long.

Even today pet turtles don't cost a lot of money. But the homes they live in do.

Turtles need a lot of care. People
with turtles think it's worth it. Turtles
are a pet you watch, not play with.
They can be very smart. Some will
look up at you and beg for food.
Before getting a turtle, learn
how to take care of it.

DID YOU KNOW?

There are turtles alive today that were born in the 1800s.

All About Turtles

Turtles lived alongside dinosaurs. They have been on this planet for more than 200 million years. An early turtle called "Odontochelys" (oh-DON-toe-KELL-iss) lived where China is today. It had teeth and just half a shell.

Turtles are reptiles. They are **cold-blooded**. They lay eggs.

The words turtle, tortoise, and terrapin are often used **interchangeably**; however, they have many differences. Tortoises live mainly on land.

Turtles prefer the water. Terrapins enjoy both.

A turtle's shell is made of bone. It's connected to the turtle. They can't slip out of it. Scared turtles tuck their head, legs and tail into the shell. Land turtles have sturdy legs with short feet and claws on the toes. Sea turtles have flippers instead of front feet.

Turtles no longer have teeth. They have beaks like parrots.

There are over 250 turtle **species**. Turtles can be a few inches long. The Atlantic Leatherback turtle is over seven feet long. It weighs more than 1,500 pounds. Not every turtle makes a good pet. Some are too big. Some are too mean. You need to find the right turtle for you.

The Right Turtle

Baby Red-eared sliders are very cute. Just a few inches long, they are also pretty fast—for a turtle. They are easy to feed. They are happy living indoors with people. They are the most **popular** pet turtles in the U.S.

They also get big. Adult sliders can be over one foot long. Wild Red-eared sliders once lived mainly along the Mississippi River. Unfortunately, people with large pet sliders let them go. Today the turtles can be found all over the U.S., along with parts of Asia and Europe. They are often spotted in New York City's Central Park.

You can tell these turtles by the red streak on each side of their head. They have webbed feet with sharp claws. Babies have greenish shells. To take care of a slider you will need a very large turtle tank.

DID YOU KNOW?

Since 1975, it has been against the law to sell turtles with shells less than four inches long.

The smaller Painted turtle might be a better choice. They got their name because their shells look like someone just painted them. Adults are around six inches long. This means they don't need as large a tank as sliders. They are lively even as adults. They love swimming and are very active. They like watching their owners.

Other pet turtles include the tiny Eastern box turtle, the Wood turtle, and the Map turtle. Every turtle has different needs. Learn about those needs before you bring one home. Make sure you have a place set up for them.

Your Turtle's Home

Pet turtles can live a very long life. Yet many do better in the wild. Why? The main reason is their **environment**.

Every type of turtle needs a different **habitat**. Red-eared sliders live in ponds, swamps, and slow rivers. Pet sliders need a large **aquarium**. Buy one made to hold water. Fish tanks work well. You will need a heater to keep the water warm. The water should be kept at 75 degrees Fahrenheit. Make sure the heater is stainless steel or protected by a plastic cage. *Turtles can break glass heaters and that is very dangerous.*

Multiply your turtle's length in inches by 10. This is the number of gallons your tank will need to be. Large turtles need a 75 to 100-gallon tank. It should be long enough for the turtle to swim. It must be deeper than the turtle's width. This is in case your turtle gets turned upside-down. Your turtle should be able to easily flip over. If it can't do this, it can drown.

Fill the tank with water about three inches from the top. Your turtle's home is also its bathroom. Its water needs to be changed often. Use a good **filtration** system to keep the water from getting dirty. Dirty water makes turtles sick. Buy filters made for a larger tank. If your tank is forty gallons, get an 80-gallon filter.

Soft-shelled turtles need a layer of sand on the bottom of the tank. Other turtles don't. Keep the tank clean. Don't add gravel. Do give your little guy a place to climb out of the water. This can be a rock or a piece of driftwood. It needs to be above the water line. Your turtle should be able to climb up and out. You can also get a **basking** spot that floats.

Wild turtles love lying in the sun. Remember, they are cold-blooded. They need heat to stay warm. Indoors, your pet turtle will use a basking bulb. This bulb is like the sun. It should reach 80 degrees Fahrenheit. Put the bulb by the piece of driftwood, rock or another basking spot. Don't place it too close to where the turtle will be. Your turtle might need a ramp to get in and out of the water.

When your turtle home is ready, it's time to get your turtle!

DID YOU KNOW?

Contrary to popular belief, a turtle cannot come out of its shell. The turtle's shell grows with them, so it's impossible for them to grow too big for it!

Getting Your Turtle

Pet turtles are still shipped in the mail. It is not a good idea to order a turtle online. The only way to make sure a turtle is happy and healthy is by spending time with it.

Turtles can be found at pet stores. There are also turtle **breeders**. They offer special types of turtles. Turtles from pet stores and breeders are used to eating turtle food. They are used to living in a turtle tank.

The best turtle might be a turtle someone else did not want. Red-eared sliders often wind up with rescue groups when they get too big. **Adopting** a pet turtle might be the best choice.

Spend some time with the turtle. Healthy turtles are surprisingly quick. They might move around to keep from getting picked up. Their eyes should be clear. A slider's shell is hard. Soft spots mean it might be sick.

Do NOT take a turtle you found in your backyard. It might be **endangered**. It is against the law to take a turtle from the wild. Plus, you could be bringing a disease into your home.

DID YOU KNOW?

In Florida, it has been illegal to buy or sell Red-eared sliders since 2007.

Turtle Time

Every turtle is different. Some turtle owners say their turtles will come when their name is called. Others have turtles that perk up when it is time to eat.

Most turtles do not like to be picked up. Before you touch your turtle, always wash your hands. Wash your hands afterward, too. Never put part of a turtle in your mouth or put your fingers in your mouth while you are handling a turtle. Turtles can carry salmonella. Salmonella on food can make you very sick. It can make you just as sick when it is on a turtle.

When you hold a turtle, let its bottom shell rest on the palm of your hand. This way when its legs are out, its feet have somewhere to go. Turtles don't like to be grabbed by the top part of the shell. It isn't a good idea to hold them so their legs dangle.

Give your turtle time to get to know you. Let it come to you. Some turtles will even rest their heads on your feet.

DID YOU KNOW?
World Turtle Day is on May 23rd every year.

Turtle Diet

Young turtles are **carnivores**. They eat mainly meat. Older turtles eat more plants. Like most humans, they are **omnivorous**. It means they like meat and their veggies.

Turtles become adults when they are seven-years old. Adult turtles should be fed four to five times per week. Younger turtles eat every day.

Turtle pellets are sold at pet stores. Get ones made for your type of turtle. Pellets float.

Don't overfeed your turtle! An adult only needs one cup of food. One quarter of this should be pellets. Half the cup can be chopped dark leafy greens like kale. You can also give them sliced squash and carrots. Have an adult help you chop the veggies. A sliced bit of apple is a nice treat. You can put the greens right in the water.

You can also use a feeding cup that will stick to the side of the tank.

Turtles also eat insects, earthworms and feeder fish like comet goldfish. Keep their water fresh. Turtles drink the water they live in. Giving them a variety of food is one way to keep them healthy.

At the Vets

Turtles are not like most pets. You don't need to walk them. They are terrible at fetch. Most get enough play and exercise in their tank.

The best way to keep your turtle healthy is to visit a **veterinarian**. These are doctors for animals. Not every vet takes turtles. You will want to find one that knows how to keep reptiles healthy. Have a vet check out your turtle as soon as you can.

A vet can spot things you can't. The doctor can check your turtle for roundworms. These creatures can make your turtle very sick.

As you and your turtle become friends, you will notice when she isn't feeling well. If she stops eating, she needs to see a vet. Wheezing or having trouble breathing are also a sign of illness. So are puffy eyes or soft places on its shell. If your slider stops diving into the water, it might be sick.

If your new turtle is a baby, make sure it has enough space as it grows.

Check its lights and heater often. Take good care of it.

Turtles are fascinating to watch, and many have attractive colors and markings, and interesting personalities. They can make great interactive pets.

SHOPPING LIST

This is a list of some things your turtle will need:

☐ A turtle tank that can hold at least 40 gallons and is four feet long. Multiply your turtle's length in inches by 10 to get the number of gallons you will need.

☐ Turtle tank filter system. Use a filter made for a larger tank. If your tank is forty gallons, get a filter made for an 80-gallon tank.

☐ A ramp to get in and out of the water.

☐ Basking bulb (look on the label to make sure it offers both UVA and UVB light)

☐ Basking area

☐ Thermometer for both the air and water

☐ Turtle pellets. Get the ones made just for your type of turtle.

FIND OUT MORE

Online
There are several sites that will help you raise a healthy and happy turtle:

How to set up your turtle tank:
https://www.myturtlecam.com/habitat.php

Learn more about adopting a pet turtle:
Turtle Rescue League
http://www.turtlerescueleague.com/about/pet-turtles/turtle-adoption

Petfinder connects people with adoptable animals. They have turtles in their "scales, skins and others" section:
https://www.petfinder.com/search/scales-fins-others-for-adoption/?sort%5B0%5D=recently_added

Books

Barr, Catherine. *10 Reasons to Love a Turtle*. New York: Frances Lincoln Children's Books. 2017.

Marsh, Laura. National Geographic Readers: Turtles Washington D.C.: *National Geographic*. 2016.

Meister, Cari. *My First Pet: Turtles.* Minneapolis, MN: Jump! 2016.

Hamilton, Lynn. *Turtle.* New York: Weigl Publishers, 2010.

GLOSSARY

adoption
Taking care of someone without a family

aquarium
A glass tank filled with water for turtles or fish

basking
To lie or relax happily in a bright and warm place

breeders
People who keep and take care of animals or plants in order to produce more animals or plants of a specific kind

carnivore
Animal that only eats meat

cold-blooded
Having a body temperature that is like the temperature of the environment

endangered
An animal or plant that is very rare and could die out completely

environment
The kind of conditions an animal lives in

filtration
Means of removing unwanted material

interchangeably
Capable of being used in place of each other

habitat
Natural home of an animal

omnivore
Animal that eats both meat and vegetables

popular
Well-liked

species
A group of similar animals

veterinarian
Doctor who specializes in animal care

BIBLIOGRAPHY

Anyangwe, Eliza. "Why are Environmentalists Putting Graffiti on Turtles?" *CNN Wire*. July 31, 2015.

Christensen, Jen. "Pet Turtles Blamed for Multi-state Salmonella Outbreak." *CNN Wire*. August 29, 2017.

Cortez, Joe. "Turtle FAQs: What Kind of Turtle Do I Have and More." petmd. https://www.petmd.com/reptile/care/evr_rp_turtle-fun-facts

Daniels, Andrew. "What Do Pet Turtles Eat?" petmd. https://www.petmd.com/reptile/nutrition/what-do-turtles-eat

Davidson, Rose. "Terrier Saves Sea Turtles." *National Geographic Kids*, March 2016.

Demas, Paul. "Keeping a Turtle? Here are Some Tips All New Turtlekeepers Need to Know." *Reptiles Magazine*. http://www.reptilesmagazine.com/Turtles-Tortoises/Turtle-Care/Keeping-a-Turtle-Here-are-Some-Tips-All-New-Turtlekeepers-Need-To-Know/

"Freshwater Turtles." Florida Fish and Wildlife Commission. https://myfwc.com/wildlifehabitats/wildlife/freshwater-turtles/

Fogel, Dave. "A History of the Pet Hatchling Aquatic Turtle Trade in the United States." *Reptiles Magazine*. http://www.reptilesmagazine.com/Turtles-Tortoises/Turtle-Care/Pet-Hatchling-Turtle-History/

Kruzer, RVT. Adrienne "Yellow-Bellied Sliders: These Aquatic Turtles are Popular Pets." *The Spruce Pets*. February 24, 2019. https://www.thesprucepets.com/yellow-bellied-sliders-1238384

McLeod, DVM. Lianne. "All About Keeping Pet Aquatic Turtles." *The Spruce Pets*. February 8, 2019. https://www.thesprucepets.com/pet-aquatic-turtles-1237254

"What Should I Feed My Red-Eared Slider Turtle?" *The Spruce Pets*. January 26, 2019. https://www.thesprucepets.com/what-should-i-feed-my-red-eared-slider-1238363

"Turtle Care Guide." *VetBabble*. March 17, 2019. https://www.vetbabble.com/reptiles/turtles/

"Responsible Pet Ownership for Kids." *VetBabble*. February 27, 2019. https://www.vetbabble.com/dogs/getting-started-dogs/responsible-pet-ownership-for-kids/

Vadala, Nick. "How Long Do Turtles Live?" petmd. https://www.petmd.com/reptile/care/how-long-do-turtles-live

Williams, Geoff. "Turtle Care 101: How to Take Care of Pet Turtles." petmd.com https://www.petmd.com/reptile/care/evr_rp_how-to-take-care-of-pet-turtles

Yong, Ed. "Heroes in a Half-shell Show How Turtles Evolved." *National Geographic*. November 26, 2008. https://www.nationalgeographic.com/science/phenomena/2008/11/26/heroes-in-a-half-shell-show-how-turtles-evolved/

INDEX

ABOUT THE AUTHOR

John Bankston

The author of over 100 books for young readers, John Bankston lives in Miami Beach, Florida with his rescue dog Astronaut. In Florida, pet turtles are often released into the wild. He hopes writing this book will help stop that and help anyone who wants to keep a pet turtle healthy for years to come.